Creepy Crawlers

Cicadas

by Lisa J. Amstutz

Gail Saunders-Smith, PhD, Consulting Editor

Consultant: Wade Harrell
Vice President
American Tarantula Society

CAPSTONE PRESS
a capstone imprint

Pebble Plus is published by Capstone Press,
1710 Roe Crest Drive, North Mankato, Minnesota 56003.
www.capstonepub.com

Library of Congress Cataloging-in-Publication Data
Amstutz, Lisa J.
Cicadas / by Lisa J. Amstutz.
p. cm.—(Pebble Plus. Creepy Crawlers)
Summary: "Learn about cicadas, including how and where they live and
how these creepy creatures are important parts of their world"—Provided by publisher.
Audience: 005-008.
Audience: K to grade 3.
Includes bibliographical references and index.
ISBN 978-1-4765-2062-9 (library binding)
ISBN 978-4765-3477-0 (eBook PDF)
1. Cicadas—Juvenile literature. I. Title.
QL527.C5a47 2014
595.7'52—dc23   2013008522

Editorial Credits
Jeni Wittrock, editor; Kyle Grenz, designer; Laura Manthe, production specialist

Photo Credits
James P. Rowan, 21; Newscom: CMSP Biology/Kent Wood, 19; Science Source: James H. Robinson, 17; Shutterstock: asharkyu, 1, Bejim, cover, Bruce MacQueen, 15, Cameramannz, 7, Chris Alcock, 9, Kirsanov Valeriy Vladimirovich, 5, 13, Liew Weng Keong, 11, Morphart Creation, 15, vlastas66, design element (throughout)

Note to Parents and Teachers

The Creepy Crawlers set supports national science standards related to biology and life science. This book describes and illustrates cicadas. The images support early readers in understanding the text. The repetition of words and phrases helps early readers learn new words. This book also introduces early readers to subject-specific vocabulary words, which are defined in the Glossary section. Early readers may need assistance to read some words and to use the Table of Contents, Glossary, Read More, Internet Sites, and Index sections of the book.

Printed in China by Nordica.
0413/CA21300494
032013   007226NORDF13

Table of Contents

All Abuzz 4

Cicada Homes 6

Body Parts 8

A Cicada's Life 14

Glossary 22

Read More 23

Internet Sites 23

Index 24

All Abuzz

Bzzz. Bzzz.

What is making that

loud noise? It's a cicada.

Cicadas are the loudest

insects in the world.

Cicada Homes

Cicadas live in temperate or tropical climates. They are found in parts of North and South America, Asia, Europe, Africa, and Australia.

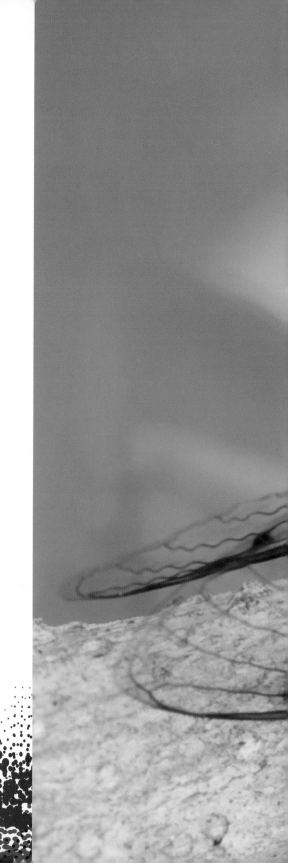

Body Parts

A big, creepy body is perfect for a cicada. Four clear wings help it fly high in the trees. All cicadas have six legs. Young cicadas have strong front legs to dig and climb.

Cicadas have five eyes.
Two eyes are large and three
are small. They look for danger
and food. Two short antennae
help cicadas find plants to eat.

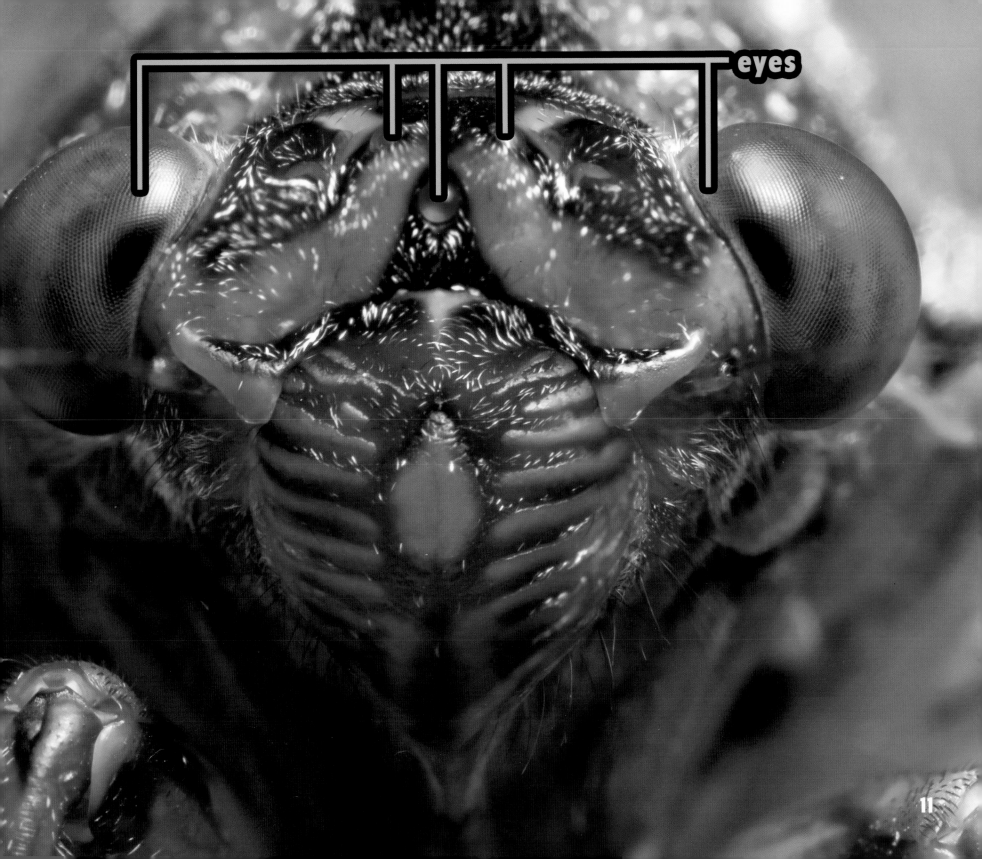

eyes

A cicada's mouth is like a straw.

The cicada pokes a hole in

a tree. It sucks out a liquid

called sap.

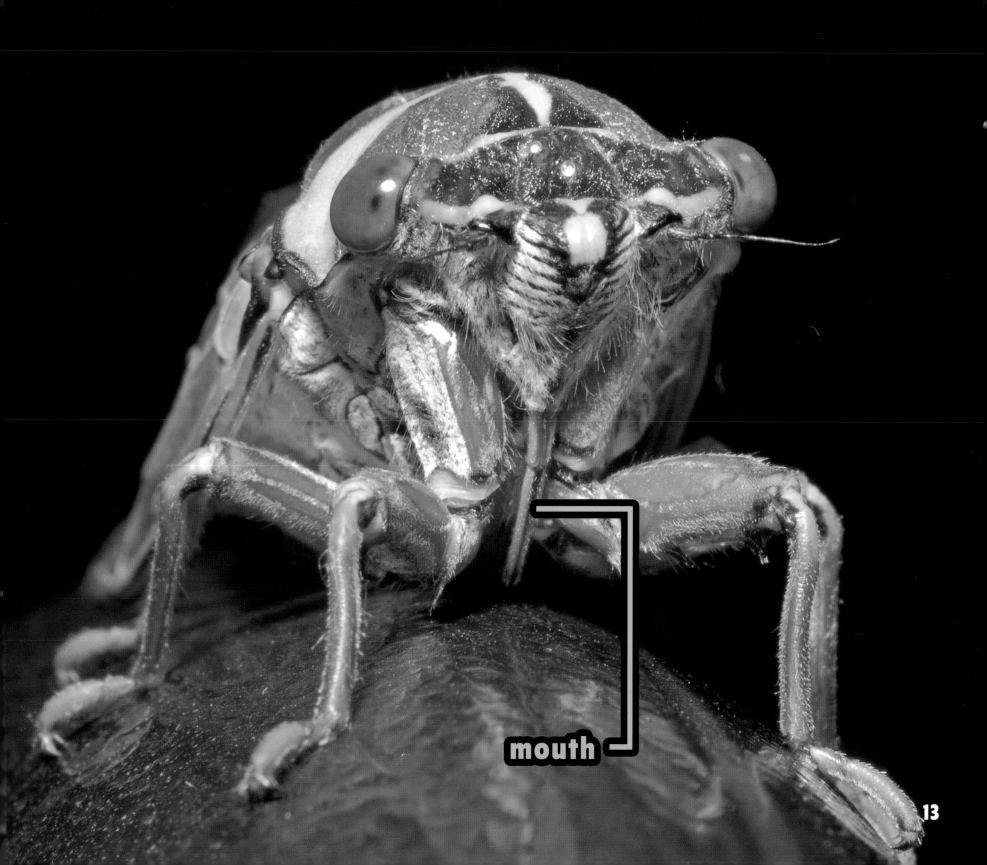

mouth

A Cicada's Life

Male cicadas buzz to call females to mate. Little drums on their bodies called tymbals make sounds. The drums pop in and out.

tymbals
under wing

After mating, a female cicada
sticks her egg-layer in a twig.
She lays about 400 eggs.
The baby cicadas, or nymphs,
hatch and fall to the ground.

egg

cut in twig

Most cicada nymphs burrow for two to three years. One type of cicada lives underground for up to 17 years! All at once, cicada nymphs come out of the ground.

The nymphs shed their old skins to become adults. You can find their empty skins on the sides of trees. Cicadas are creepy but cool!

21

Glossary

antenna—a feeler on an animal's head

burrow—to dig a hole in the ground

climate—average weather of a place throughout the year

hatch—to break out of an egg

mate—to join with another to produce young

nymph—a young cicada; nymphs change into adults by shedding their skin; cicada nymphs live underground for 2 to 17 years

sap—a fluid found inside plants and trees

shed—to drop or fall off; nymphs shed their old skin to become adults

temperate—not too hot, cold, or wet; places between the polar zones and tropical zones are temperate

tropical—hot and wet; places near the equator are tropical

tymbal—a part of an insect's body that vibrates to make sound

Read More

Himmelman, John. *Noisy Bug Sing-Along.*
Nevada City, Calif.: Dawn Publications, 2013.

Pringle, Laurence. *Cicadas!: Strange and Wonderful.*
Honesdale, Penn.: Boyds Mills Press, 2010.

Roza, Greg. *The Bizarre Life Cycle of a Cicada.* Strange
Life Cycles. New York: Gareth Stevens Pub., 2012.

Internet Sites

FactHound offers a safe, fun way to find Internet sites
related to this book. All of the sites on FactHound have
been researched by our staff.

Here's all you do:

Visit *www.facthound.com*

Type in this code: 9781476520629

Super-cool stuff! Check out projects, games and lots more at
www.capstonekids.com

Index

adults, 20

antennae, 10

burrowing, 18

buzzing, 4, 14

climbing, 8

digging, 8

eating, 10, 12

eggs, 16

eyes, 10

females, 14, 16

food, 10

hatching, 16

homes, 6

legs, 8

males, 14

mouths, 12

noises, 4

nymphs, 16, 18

shedding, 20

tymbals, 14

wings, 8

young, 8

Word Count: 229
Grade: 1
Early-Intervention Level: 18